This Is a Let's-Read-and-Find-Out Science Book®
REVISED EDITION

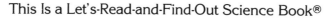

MILK
FROM COW TO CARTON

by Aliki

HarperCollins*Publishers*

For Ruedi and Annemarie, Oskar and Ruth,
Erich and Barbara, Herbert and Iris,
and all the children

With thanks to Joseph Kagan and Franz Xaver Albisser for their help

The illustrations for this book were done on watercolor board, using a combination of ink, watercolors, and pencil crayons.

The *Let's-Read-and-Find-Out Science Book* series was originated by Dr. Franklyn M. Branley, Astronomer Emeritus and former Chairman of the American Museum–Hayden Planetarium, and was formerly co-edited by him and Dr. Roma Gans, Professor Emeritus of Childhood Education, Teachers College, Columbia University. For a complete catalog of Let's-Read-and-Find-Out Science Books, write to HarperCollins Children's Books, 10 East 53rd Street, New York, NY 10022.

Let's-Read-and-Find-Out Science Book is a registered trademark of HarperCollins Publishers.

Library of Congress Cataloging-in-Publication Data
Aliki.
    Milk from cow to carton / by Aliki. — Rev. ed.
        p.   cm. — (Let's-read-and-find-out science book)
    Rev. ed. of: Green grass and white milk. 1974.
    Summary: Briefly describes how a cow produces milk, how the milk is processed in a dairy, and how various other dairy products are made from milk.
    ISBN 0-06-020434-6. — ISBN 0-06-020435-4 (lib. bdg.)
    ISBN 0-06-445111-9 (pbk.)
    1. Dairying—Juvenile literature.   2. Milk—Juvenile literature. 3. Cows—Juvenile literature. [1. Dairying.   2. Milk.   3. Cows.]
I. Aliki. Green grass and white milk.   II. Title.   III. Series.
SF239.5.A45   1992   91-23807
637—dc20   CIP
                                                                            AC

MILK
FROM COW TO CARTON

In the warm spring and summer
cows graze high in the mountains.
They graze in valleys, in fields, and in meadows.
They eat and eat in good green pastures.

Nearby a farmer and his helpers cut grass.
They dry it in the sun.
They are making hay for the cold days ahead.

In winter a cow stays in the barn, snug and warm.
She eats the hay.
Good summer grass and good winter hay
are healthy food for a cow.
The better a cow eats, the better the milk she will give.

When a cow eats, she tears the grass off
with her tongue and teeth.
She swallows her food quickly.
She does not chew it well.
The food is stored in the first or second of her four stomachs.
That's right! A cow has four stomachs.
Later, when a cow has finished eating,
she lies quietly and chews her food again.
She brings up bits of unchewed food—or cud—
from her stomach.
She chews her cud properly, a little at a time.
It looks as if she is chewing gum.
Then she swallows it again.

9

After a cow swallows all her cud, stomachs
number three and four digest the food even better.
Then part of the food is made into milk.
The rest is nourishment for the cow.

A cow's four stomachs are: 1. Rumen   2. Reticulum   3. Omasum   3. Abomasum

A. Unchewed food goes into stomachs 1 and 2.
B. Unchewed food (cud) is brought back up to be chewed well.
C. Well-chewed food goes into stomachs 3 and 4.
D. Part of the food is made into milk.

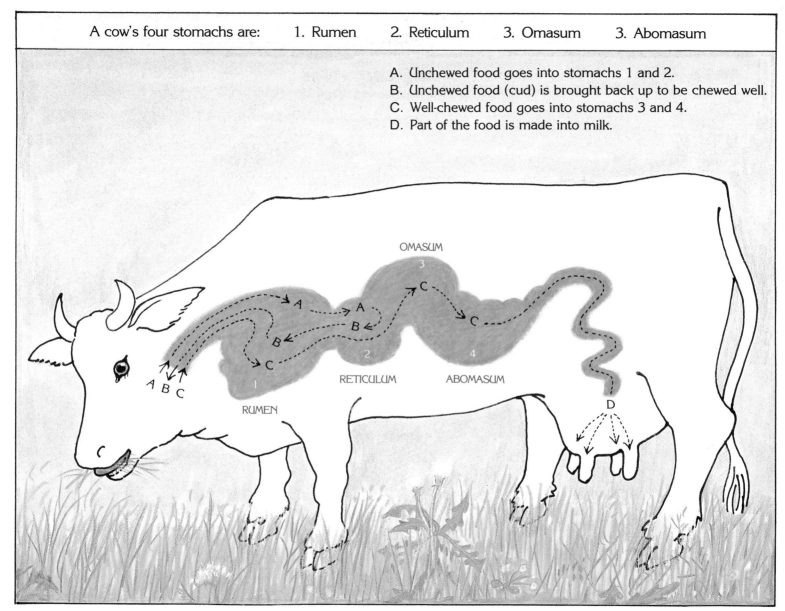

A cow begins to make milk when she has a calf.
The milk is food for the newborn calf.
A cow has milk even after her calf needs it.
Once the calf starts eating grass, the cow's milk
can become food for us.
Cows produce lots of milk.
A healthy, contented cow can give thirty quarts a day.

Last summer my brother and I visited a farm
high up in the mountains.
The dark, damp barn smelled of straw and cows.
It smelled so much, I had to hold my nose.
Then I got used to the smell and liked it.

It was milking time.
A cow is milked twice a day—
early morning and late afternoon.
We watched.

15

Milk is made and stored in the cow's udder.
The udder is a bag with four teats.
By milking time the udder is full.
When a teat is squeezed, milk flows out.

The farmer washed the cow's teats.
Then he squeezed them.
He squirted some milk into a cup, and we tasted a sip.
The raw milk was warm and good.
Then we watched the farmer milk his cows.
He kept a record of how much milk each one gave.

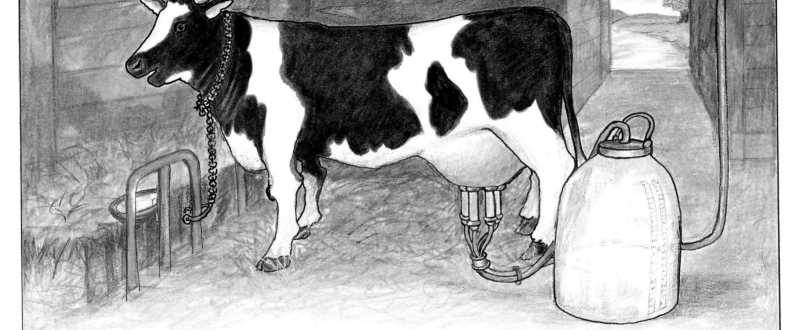

Farmers with many cows use a machine to milk faster.
A milking machine has four cups that fit onto the cow's teats.
The milk is pumped through tubes into a covered pail.
Milking never hurts the cow.
She feels comfortable afterward.

Raw milk from the cows is stored in a refrigerated tank. Every day that milk is pumped into a big refrigerated tanker and taken to the dairy.

LAB TECHNICIAN
(tests milk sample)

RAW MILK

A dairy is where the raw milk is processed.
In a dairy there are big tanks to store the milk.
There are pipes for the milk to flow through.
There are machines to homogenize and pasteurize the milk,
and machines to put it into bottles and cartons.

A dairy is a very clean place.
The floors and walls are spotless.
The pipes, tanks, and machines are washed
inside and out every night.
You never have to hold your nose in a dairy.

HOW MILK IS PROCESSED

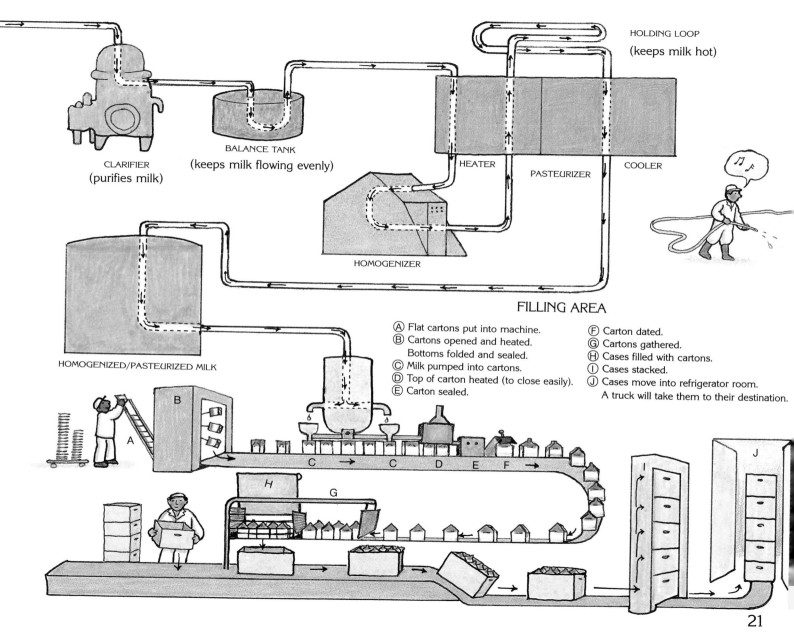

CLARIFIER
(purifies milk)

BALANCE TANK
(keeps milk flowing evenly)

HEATER

PASTEURIZER

COOLER

HOLDING LOOP
(keeps milk hot)

HOMOGENIZER

HOMOGENIZED/PASTEURIZED MILK

FILLING AREA

Ⓐ Flat cartons put into machine.
Ⓑ Cartons opened and heated.
   Bottoms folded and sealed.
Ⓒ Milk pumped into cartons.
Ⓓ Top of carton heated (to close easily).
Ⓔ Carton sealed.

Ⓕ Carton dated.
Ⓖ Cartons gathered.
Ⓗ Cases filled with cartons.
Ⓘ Cases stacked.
Ⓙ Cases move into refrigerator room.
   A truck will take them to their destination.

21

When the milk is brought to the dairy, a sample
is tested immediately.
In the laboratory the milk is checked for freshness.
It is checked for butterfat.
Butterfat is the cream that rises to the top of the milk
if it is left to stand.
The creamier the milk, the more a farmer is paid for it.

If the milk passes inspection, the processing begins.
Most of the milk is homogenized in a machine.
Homogenized means "made the same all the way through."
The butterfat is broken up into tiny bits.
It is mixed into the rest of the milk.
The butterfat no longer rises to the top of the milk as cream.

Homogenized whole milk is rich and creamy.
Some people think it is too creamy.
They can drink milk processed in other ways.
Skimmed milk has all the cream taken out.
Other milks have only some of the cream taken out.
The cream is packaged separately.

Milk is heated and cooled down as it flows through the pasteurizer.

After it has been homogenized, the milk
is pasteurized to kill any bad germs.
The milk is heated quickly until it almost boils.
Then it is quickly cooled again.
Pasteurization was invented by Louis Pasteur.

Louis Pasteur (1822-1895), the French scientist, became famous when he found a way to rid milk of dangerous germs.

After milk has been processed, it is poured into bottles and cartons.
Each is labeled with the kind of milk inside.
What kind do you drink?

Other products are made from milk in a dairy, too.

Milk and dairy products contain protein, vitamins, and minerals, such as calcium, that give you energy and make you strong.

Most of the milk we drink comes from cows.
But all mammals give milk.
In some countries where there aren't many cows,
people drink the milk of goats and sheep.

Farmers make cheese from these milks, too.

You can be a dairy farmer right in your kitchen
and make your own butter.
You can make butter by hand or in an electric mixer.
Pour a pint of heavy cream into a bowl.
Beat it hard.

First it will turn into thick whipped cream.
Keep beating, and it will change again.
The whipped cream will separate
into butterfat
and a liquid called whey.
Pour out the whey—and you have butter!

It's odd. I know milk comes from cows
and other animals that eat grass.
But grass is green and milk is white.
I wonder how this happens, don't you?

I wonder.